How do you think medicines were made before there were labs and factories?

Echinacea (ek-ih-NAY-shuh) flowers grow in fields and gardens. People take medicines made from echinacea plants to feel better when they have a cold.

A Special Garden

Hundreds of years ago, medicines weren't made in labs and factories.

In many parts of the world, sick people would visit an **apothecary**.

An apothecary made medicines using plants and other ingredients.

Most apothecaries had a garden where they grew the plants for their recipes.

They sold their medicines as potions, which people drank, and as ointments.

This painting from the 1400s shows workers in an apothecary's garden.

This modern-day garden looks similar to an apothecary's garden.

The treatments made by apothecaries didn't only include plants. Sometimes they included ingredients such as mud, honey, boiled worms, and even human blood.

This wooden box contains a beehive where bees make honey.

Making Medicines

Apothecaries used roots, stems, leaves, flowers, and seeds in their medicines.

They made an **antiseptic** using colorful calendula flowers.

This medicine was put on cuts, bee stings, and dog bites.

They also boiled the roots of comfrey plants to make a paste.

Cloth was soaked in the paste and wrapped around broken bones to heal them.

calendula flower

Apothecaries used a tool called a mortar and pestle to grind up plants.

Hundreds of years ago, it was common for people to have fleas and lice. Apothecaries made an oil from lavender flowers that people rubbed on their bodies to kill these insects.

Tea for Healing

Many plants used by apothecaries are still used today, such as peppermint.

The bright green peppermint plant is an **herb**.

Peppermint gives a minty flavor to some desserts, toothpastes, and chewing gum.

Mint leaves can also be used to treat stomachaches. How?

The fresh or dried leaves are put into hot water and made into a minty tea.

What plant, which makes food taste hot and spicy, do you think is used to heal aching joints?

People who have trouble sleeping can drink chamomile tea to help them doze off. To make this soothing tea, chamomile flowers are dried, crumbled up, and put into hot water.

Soothing Ointments

Some plants can be used to make soothing ointments.

Chili peppers contain a chemical that makes them taste spicy and feel hot.

This chemical is used in ointments that are rubbed on aching joints such as knees.

Another healing plant is aloe vera.

The gel-like flesh inside its pointy leaves is cooling and soothing.

The gel is rubbed onto the skin to treat sunburns and stings.

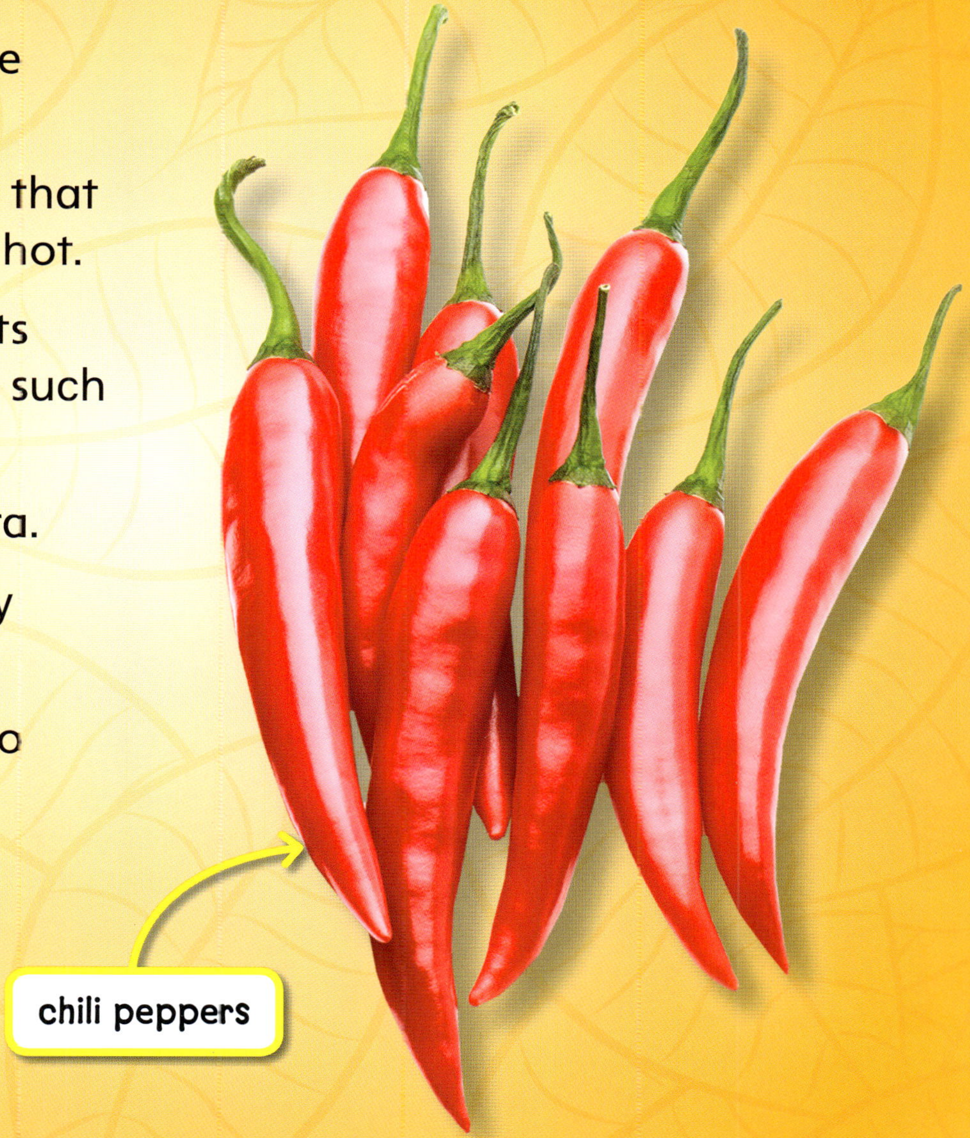

Aloe vera gel is not only healing for humans but for animals, too. Vets and pet owners can use the gel to treat sores on an animal's skin.

Medicine from Trees

It's not only small plants that can heal—trees can, too.

Native Americans once collected bark from willow trees.

They shredded the bark and mixed it with hot water to make a drink.

This drink was used as a fever reducer and as a painkiller to treat headaches and toothaches.

Willow bark is still used today to make pain medicines.

bark on the trunk of a willow tree

Willow bark contains a chemical called salicin. In the late 1800s, scientists discovered how to use salicin to make aspirin. Today, people around the world take aspirin as a painkiller and to help treat heart problems.

Ginkgo Trees

There's another tree, found in many cities around the world, that can help heal people.

The leaves of ginkgo trees contain a chemical that helps improve brain function.

The leaves are dried and made into pills.

People take these pills to help strengthen their memories.

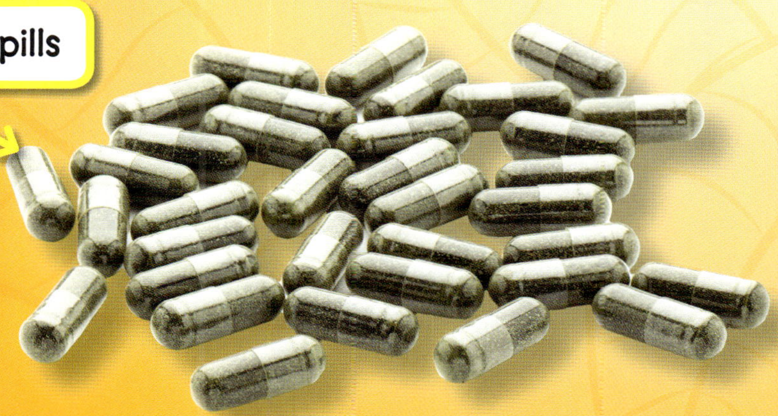

Where would be a good place to look for new types of healing plants?

Ginkgo is also used to help people with a disease called Alzheimer's. This disease usually affects older people and causes them to lose their memories.

ginkgo trees in a city in Japan

Rain Forest Medicines

Rain forests are home to more than 170,000 different types of plants!

People who live in South American rain forests have been healing with plants for hundreds of years.

They use the cat's claw plant to treat pain and skin **infections**.

Juices from the jambu plant are used to cure toothaches.

A man from the Mentawai tribe in Indonesia searches for healing plants in a rain forest.

Scientists believe there could be thousands of new plants still to be discovered in rain forests. Many of these plants may contain chemicals that could treat and cure illnesses.

A Flower That Saves Lives

One rain forest plant from the African island of Madagascar has even been used to treat cancer.

For years, many children died from a type of cancer called leukemia.

In the 1950s, scientists discovered that the Madagascar periwinkle contains a cancer-fighting chemical.

Now, medicines made with this plant save the lives of thousands of children each year!

Madagascar periwinkle

It's not only humans that use rain forest plants as mecicines. Orangutans eat serantung flowers to treat heacaches. They also chew up commelina leaves and rub the spitty mixture onto their bodies to heal aches and pains.

an orangutan in a rain forest in Indonesia

commelina plant

Science Lab

A Healing Plants Book

Make your own book to teach friends and family members about healing plants.

Include the plants from this book that you think are the most interesting.

You can also use the Internet to learn about other healing plants.

How to Make Your Book

1. Have an adult staple two pieces of paper together.
2. Write the name of a healing plant at the top of each page.
3. Research facts about each plant.
4. Then write two or three sentences about each one and draw pictures to illustrate the facts.
5. Share your book with friends and family members.

Think about these questions when you are researching healing plants. Include the answers in your information.

- **Which part of the plant is used to make a medicine?**
- **How does this plant help heal people?**

Science Words

antiseptic (an-tih-SEP-tik) a medicine that stops germs from spreading and causing disease

apothecary (uh-POTH-ih-kare-ee) a person from the past who made and sold medicines made from plants and other ingredients

herb (ERB) a plant with roots, stems, leaves, flowers, or seeds that are used to flavor food or to make medicines or perfumes

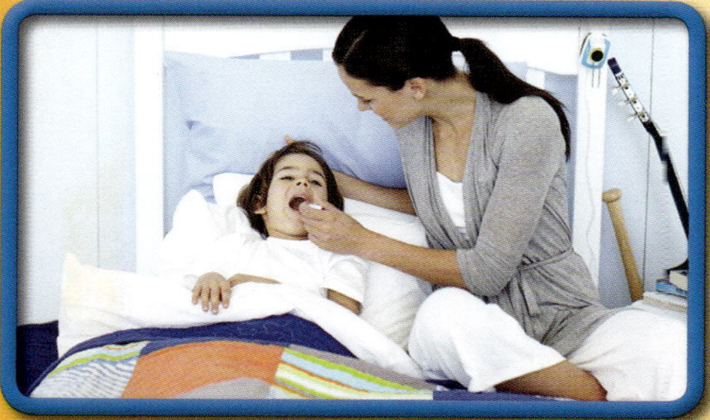

infections (in-FEK-shuhnz) illnesses caused by germs entering the body

ointments (OINT-mihnts) thick liquids or creams that are rubbed on the body to soothe pain or fight infections

rain forests (RAYN FOR-ists) warm places where many trees grow and lots of rain falls

Index

Read More

Cooper, Sharon Katz. *Using Plants (Exploring Earth's Resources)*. Chicago: Heinemann (2007).

Lawrence, Ellen. *Prickly Plants: Stuck! (Plant-ology)*. New York: Bearport (2013).

Morgan, Sally. *How We Use Plants for Medicine and Health (How We Use Plants)*. New York: Rosen (2009).

Learn More Online

To learn more about healing plants, visit
www.bearportpublishing.com/Plant-ology

About the Author

Ellen Lawrence lives in the United Kingdom. Her favorite books to write are those about nature and animals. In fact, the first book Ellen bought for herself, when she was six years old, was the story of a gorilla named Patty Cake that was born in New York's Central Park Zoo.

Medicine from a Garden?

Achoo! Ouch!

When people are sick or hurt, they might visit a pharmacy.

The pills and **ointments** sold at these stores are made in labs and factories.

Did you know that some of the ingredients in medicines come from plants?

These plants can be found growing in meadows, forests, and gardens.

So which plants are used to heal us? Let's investigate!

a pharmacy

Contents

Credits

Cover, © anyaivanova/Shutterstock; 3L, © Mrs Ya/Shutterstock; 3TR, © Nattika/Shutterstock; 3BR, © joloei/Shutterstock; 4T, © 2xSamara.com/Shutterstock; 4B, © Fuse/Thinkstock; 5, © gengirl/Shutterstock; 6, © The Print Collector/Alamy; 7, © Erica Olson/FLPA; 8T, © voranat/Shutterstock; 8B, © Swapan Photography/Shutterstock; 9L, © Radka Palenikova/Shutterstock; 9BL, © WILDLIFE GmbH/Alamy; 9BR, © LiliGraphie/Shutterstock; 10T, © lzf/Shutterstock; 10B, © viki2win/Shutterstock; 11, © Vahan Abrahamyan/Shutterstock; 11BR, © Whiteaster/Shutterstock; 12, © Nattika/Shutterstock; 13, © anyaivanova/Shutterstock; 13R, © crystalfcto/Shutterstock; 14, © Wojciech Lisinski/Shutterstock; 15L, © diane555/IstockPhoto; 15, © Jessie Eldora Robertson/Shutterstock; 16T, © azure1/Shutterstock; 16B, © Gita Kulinitch Studio/Shutterstock; 17, © Cowardlion/Shutterstock; 18T, © Amazon-Images MBSI/Alamy; 18B, © H. Zell; 19, © epa european pressphoto agency b.v./Alamy; 20T, © Apichad nakat/Shutterstock; 20B, © joloei/Shutterstock; 21, © Matej Hudovernik/Shutterstock; 21BR, © Rob Hainer/Shutterstock; 22, © ecco/Shutterstock; 23TL, © Image Point Fr/Shutterstock; 23TC, © The Print Collector/Alamy; 23TR, © Africa Studio/Shutterstock; 23BL, © wavebreakmedia/Shutterstock; 23BC, © Africa Studio/Shutterstock; 23BR, © Frank Vassen.

Publisher: Kenn Goin
Editor: Jessica Rudolph
Creative Director: Spencer Brinker
Design: Emma Randall
Photo Researcher: Ruby Tuesday Books Ltd

Library of Congress Cataloging-in-Publication Data

Lawrence, Ellen, 1967– author.
Healing plants : medicine from nature / by Ellen Lawrence.
pages cm. — (Plant-ology)
Audience: Ages 7–12.
Summary: "In this book, readers learn which plants can help make people feel better."— Provided by publisher.
Includes bibliographical references and index.
ISBN 978-1-62724-866-2 (library binding) — ISBN 1-62724-866-8 (library binding)
— ISBN 978-1-64280-795-0 (pbk.)
1. Medicinal plants—Juvenile literature. 2. Materia medica, Vegetable—Juvenile literature. I. Title.
QK99.A1L39 2016
581.6'34—dc23

2015017882

For more information, write to Bearport Publishing, 5357 Penn Avenue South, Minneapolis MN 55419.
Printed in the United States of America.

Plant-ology

Healing Plants

Medicine from Nature

by Ellen Lawrence

Consultant:

Michael Holland
Head of Education
Chelsea Physic Garden, London

BEARPORT PUBLISHING

New York, New York